SPOTLIGHT ON THE CIVIL RIGHTS MOVEMENT™

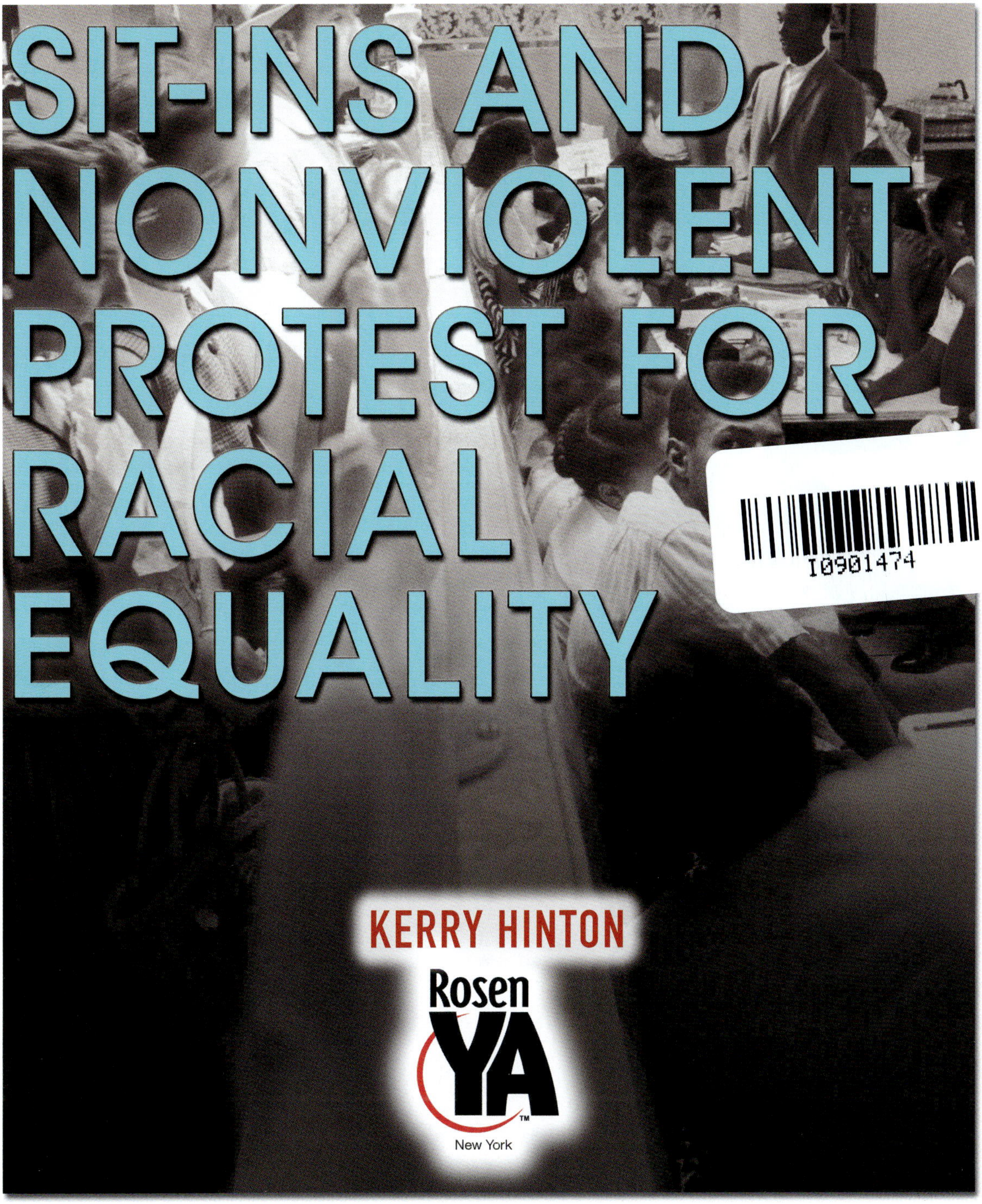

SIT-INS AND NONVIOLENT PROTEST FOR RACIAL EQUALITY

KERRY HINTON

Rosen YA™
New York

Published in 2018 by The Rosen Publishing Group, Inc.
29 East 21st Street, New York, NY 10010

First Edition

Library of Congress Cataloging-in-Publication Data

Names: Hinton, Kerry, author.
Title: Sit-ins and nonviolent protest for racial equality / Kerry Hinton.
Description: New York, NY : Rosen Publishing, 2018 | Series: Spotlight on the civil rights movement | Includes bibliographical references and index. | Audience: Grades 5–10.
Identifiers: LCCN 2017016804| ISBN 9781538380673 (library bound) | ISBN 9781538380642 (pbk.) | ISBN 9781538380659 (6 pack)
Subjects: LCSH: African Americans—Civil rights—Southern States—History—20th century—Juvenile literature. | Civil rights demonstrations—Southern States—History—20th century—Juvenile literature. | Civil rights movements—Southern States—History—20th century—Juvenile literature. | Freedom Rides, 1961—Juvenile literature. | African American civil rights workers—Southern States—History—20th century—Juvenile literature. | Civil rights workers—Southern States—History—20th century—Juvenile literature. | Southern States—Race relations—History—20th century—Juvenile literature.
Classification: LCC E185.61 .H66 2018 | DDC 323.1196/0730750904—dc23
LC record available at https://lccn.loc.gov/2017016804

Manufactured in the United States of America

On the cover: Cafeterias, lunch counters in restaurants, and peaceful marches became means of protest during the civil rights movement.

CONTENTS

WHAT IS NONVIOLENT PROTEST?

Throughout the history of the world, people have always disagreed. In many cases, members of groups of the same race, religion, or sex have been moved to confront unfair social conditions. If discussion and compromise fail to correct inequality, people are sometimes forced to take action to change their circumstances. When two opposing views cannot agree on a solution, violence can be a direct result.

There is a way to be heard without using violent action, however—nonviolent resistance. Nonviolent resistance allows people to protest peacefully against injustice. It includes picketing (gathering in a place to protest), boycotts (refusing to shop at a busi-

Many forms of peaceful protest can be used to bring attention to social conditions that may need to be changed.

ness or use a service), strikes (refusing to work until a problem is addressed), civil disobedience (refusing to comply with laws or pay taxes or fines until an injustice is addressed), and sit-ins (staying at a business until service is given). All of these techniques are types of nonviolent resistance.

Gandhi's philosophy of nonviolence inspired generations of activists to use peaceful protest to confront much larger organizations.

One of the most famous nonviolent protesters of the twentieth century was an Indian lawyer named Mahatma Gandhi (1869–1948). In 1947, Gandhi was a leader in the fight to end forty-nine years of British rule over India. He started a nonviolent movement called satyagraha (pronounced SAH-tee-AH-grah-HA) to accomplish this. Satyagraha means "clinging to truth" in Sanskrit. Gandhi led marches and served time in prison to show the British Empire how much he and his people believed in their position. Their civil disobedience helped India break free of the British Empire, unite, and govern itself. Years later, Gandhi's achievements inspired Dr. Martin Luther King Jr. and other African Americans, who eventually used nonviolent principles as part of the civil rights movement.

THE SEEDS OF THE CIVIL RIGHTS MOVEMENT

Human slavery in the United States lasted for over two hundred years. Many slaves were brought from Africa to North America. They were forced to work hard long days for no pay. Their living conditions were harsh. Sometimes, dozens of slaves were crammed into large rooms without beds. Many slaves lived on large farms called plantations. There, they were mostly forced to farm cotton, one of the most profitable crops in the world. Slavery was a huge part of the economy of the southern United States. Not all states were slave states. Some, such as Massachusetts and Pennsylvania, outlawed slavery as early as 1780. As time went on, many of the industrial northern states outlawed slavery. For most southern states, though, losing the free labor slavery provided was unacceptable.

Slave ships were designed to carry the maximum number of Africans to points around the world. Comfort and health were rarely considered.

Many of the senators who voted to ratify the Thirteenth Amendment favored the abolition of slavery, but not equal rights for freed slaves.

The refusal of white southerners to end the practice of slavery was a cause of the Civil War (1861–1865). The North's victory in 1865 led to the passage of the Thirteenth Amendment to the United States Constitution, which outlawed slavery throughout the country.

In order for laws to work, however, they must be enforced. Once federal troops left the South after the period following the Civil War, known as Reconstruction, many states in the South moved backwards. Many restrictions of the era of slavery returned, but with a new name: the Jim Crow system. Jim Crow not only involved segregation laws, it also kept the power structure of slavery in place, with whites on top and blacks on the bottom. Jim Crow could be used to justify almost any action, violent or not, to prevent African Americans from voting or having a voice for change.

JIM CROW: LEGAL DISCRIMINATION

Jim Crow laws lasted from the 1870s until the mid-1960s. They were designed to control almost all aspects of everyday life for African Americans in the South. One purpose was to reinforce the idea that African Americans were inferior to whites. This false viewpoint was repeated by newspapers, advertising, and even children's songs. Voting was also prohibited or made extremely difficult by these laws, which eliminated the possibility of any real change to the system by the people it harmed the most. Many whites were also fearful that living among African Americans would destroy the purity of the white race. This fear drove much of the horrible racism of Jim Crow.

Jim Crow was a type of caste system. Whites in favor of the laws considered themselves in a higher caste, or group, than blacks and other people of color.

Jim Crow laws were supported by both state governments and citizens alike. Many white Americans had no desire to share their communities with black Americans.

Under Jim Crow, African Americans were not allowed to live in the same neighborhoods, share the same public restrooms, or eat with white Americans. "Negroes not welcome" signs were a

Jim Crow laws dictated every aspect of life for blacks in the South—both work and leisure were segregated.

common sight throughout the country during this time.

Some restaurants and stores allowed black people but made them enter through separate "colored only" entrances. Although the descendants of slaves simply wanted to live free and peaceful lives, there were some white people who could not see their struggle for what it was. Before the internet, news traveled much less quickly than it does today. Many people in the United States knew very little of the daily struggles African Americans had to endure.

Blacks who broke Jim Crow laws were almost always punished, although not always by a sentence given in a court of law. The penalties included beatings, arson of homes, and sometimes death. This was a kind of terrorism designed to keep the system whites wanted in place.

THE PHILOSOPHY BEHIND SIT-INS

Sit-ins were chosen as the best means of protest because they met violence with nonviolence. With the philosophies of Gandhi as a guide, sit-ins became part of the long tradition of nonviolent action. The idea was simple. Protesters would travel to establishments that segregated or denied service to African Americans. Once inside, they would sit down and ask to be served. If they were refused, they would sit calmly until they were served or forced to leave. Outside, other supporters would use the power of picket signs to protest these businesses for the world to see.

Above all, the young people who participated in the sit-ins had to be extremely disciplined. Retaliation was forbidden—

Many peaceful lunch counter sit-ins were met with violent behavior against the protesters themselves.

fighting back would only hurt the movement and make change more difficult to achieve. Protesters could defend themselves only. They also were instructed to act, react, and often even dress the same way to show unity for their cause.

SIT-INS BEFORE THE CIVIL RIGHTS MOVEMENT

The sit-ins of the civil rights movement were not the first of their kind. African Americans had used sit-ins as early as the 1940s to address social problems. Life in the North may have offered more freedom for black Americans, but segregation could be found there as well. Many early sit-ins were not held in the South, but in northern cities such as Washington, DC, and Chicago. These early events did not receive much attention outside of the cities in which they were held. In order for news to spread widely, more organization was needed. Organizers hoped more unity would lead to more protests and more support outside of African American communities.

As chief counsel for the NAACP, Thurgood Marshall (*center*) argued for the plaintiffs in *Brown v. Board of Education*. He later became the first African American Supreme Court justice in 1967.

In 1956, the Supreme Court ruled segregation unconstitutional in the case of *Brown v. Board of Education*. Despite this, most southern states chose to ignore the ruling and continued segregating black Americans. This attitude encouraged some to test the ruling through sit-ins.

GETTING ORGANIZED: 1940–1960

Some of the civil rights organizations were formed to address issues important to the African American community. They included:

The Congress of Racial Equality (CORE). CORE was born in 1942. Its message is simple: "To bring about equality for all people regardless of race, creed, sex, age, disability, sexual orientation, religion, or ethnic background." CORE organized some of the first restaurant sit-ins in the 1940s.

The Southern Christian Leadership Conference (SCLC). The SCLC was started in 1957 after the Montgomery bus boycott that helped desegregate buses in Montgomery, Alabama. Its first president was Dr. Martin Luther King Jr.

The Student Nonviolent Coordinating Committee (SNCC). SNCC (pronounced "snick") was founded in 1960. It had a large

The gospel hymn "We Shall Overcome" became an anthem for the civil rights movement. It was spoken and sung at many events in the 1960s, including the funeral of Dr. Martin Luther King Jr.

student membership and protested segregation at restaurants, libraries, and public swimming pools. Many members of SNCC also traveled to the Deep South to register black voters during the 1960s.

THE FIRST MODERN SIT-INS

One of the earliest sit-ins was a success. On January 20, 1955, a group of students in Baltimore, Maryland, entered Read's Drug Store and requested service. They sat for thirty minutes before they got up and exited. The reaction of the company's president was impressive—two days later, he desegregated all thirty-nine stores in the area and named the sit-in as the main reason.

Not all early sit-ins had positive results. In June 1957 a group of activists went into the "whites only" section of the Royal Ice Cream Parlor in Durham, North Carolina, and ordered. All seven of the Durham protesters were arrested for trespassing, found guilty, and fined 10 dollars (75 dollars today). After losing their appeal, they were fined an additional 25 dollars (about 200

Boycotting businesses that discriminated against African Americans spread the word about the unfair practice to the community. These protests also took a financial toll on some establishments.

dollars today). The parlors were eventually desegregated six years later, but after the quick success in Baltimore, some saw this as a setback.

THE GREENSBORO SIT-INS

On February 5, 1960, four black college students ordered lunch at Woolworth's, a segregated department store in Greensboro, North Carolina. When they were refused service, they sat quietly until the store closed for the day. Many of the white patrons were not as quiet. They yelled racial slurs and threatened violence if the young men did not leave.

Several days later, the young men returned with a few hundred students and sat in again. The protests lasted until July, when Woolworth's announced that it would be ending racial segregation company wide. Fearing a loss of business, many other stores in the area followed this example. The Greensboro sit-ins were not the first of their kind, but they were reported on a

The Greensboro protests against Woolworth's spread to the company's nonsegregated stores in northern cities such as New York.

national level and brought more attention to the unfair treatment of African Americans under Jim Crow. Afterwards, more black and white Americans who believed in racial equality were inspired to take part in sit-ins across the country.

THE NASHVILLE SIT-INS

One week after the protests in North Carolina, students from Fisk University in Nashville, Tennessee, sat in at lunch counters throughout the city. Hundreds came to show their support. The protests lasted for three months and eventually included bus stations and other businesses. Groups of prosegregation whites attacked the nonviolent protesters, and later that spring a bomb was detonated at the home of a defense lawyer for many of the protesters who had been arrested at the sit-ins. Although the only violence was committed by whites who opposed the sit-ins and boycotts, only the protesters were arrested. The patience of the activists brought a great deal of media attention and began to affect the profits of some of the targeted businesses. In May 1960, many businesses throughout the city announced they were ending segregation in public places. Successes were beginning to add up for the civil rights movement.

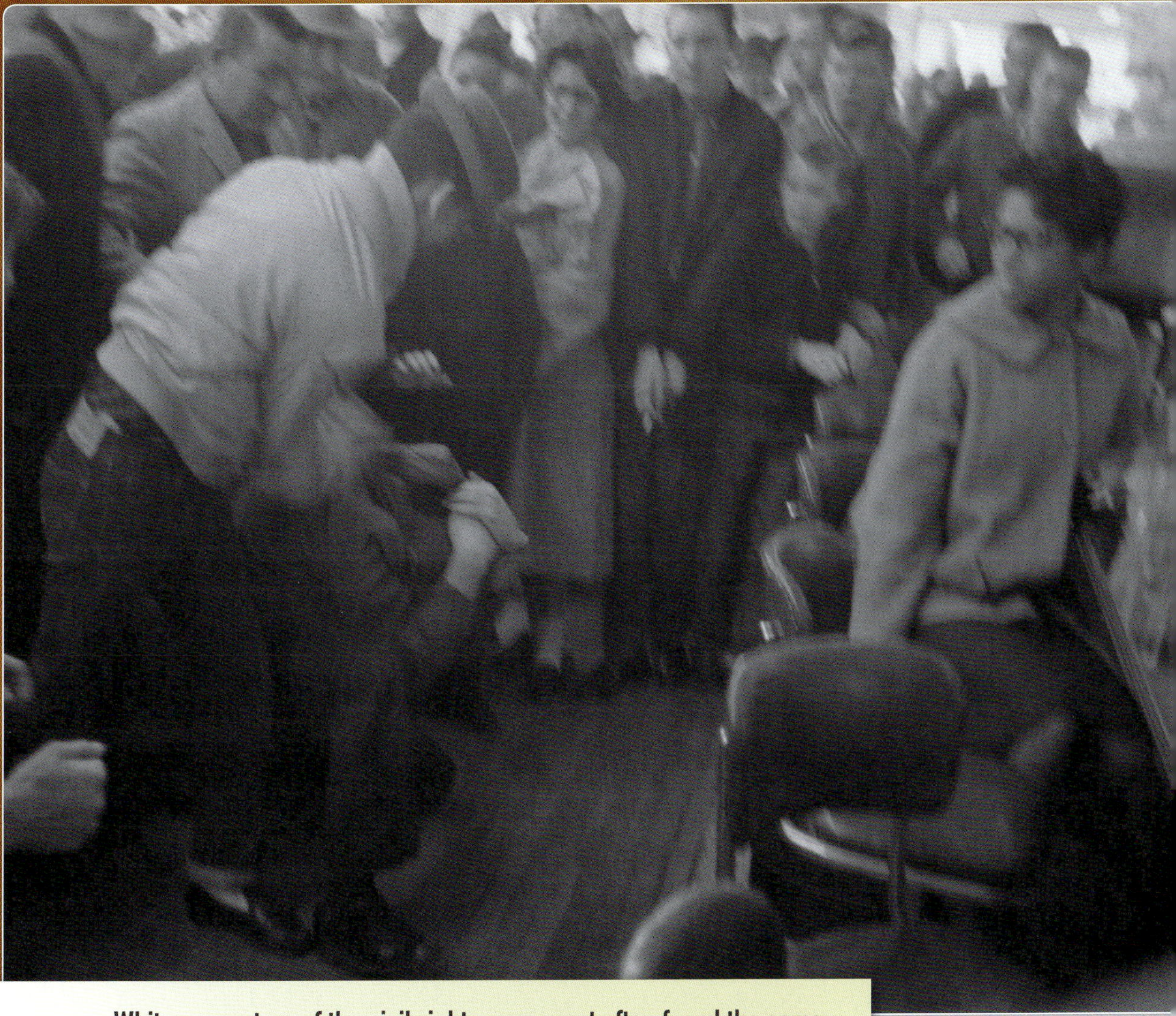

White supporters of the civil rights movement often faced the same beatings and violence as their black allies in the Jim Crow South.

THE FREEDOM RIDERS OF 1961

The Supreme Court may have outlawed segregation of public transit in 1946, but many African Americans were still forced to sit in the backs of southern buses. In 1961, brave white and black activists took to the highways to ensure the law was upheld.

The Freedom Riders left Washington, DC, in May 1961 for New Orleans, Louisiana, to mark the seventh anniversary of the *Brown v. Board of Education* decision. One week later, the riders were attacked at a bus station's whites-only waiting area. The violence increased in Aniston, Alabama. There, a Freedom Rider bus was attacked by a mob, and someone in the crowd threw a

During the Freedom Rides, buses often required the protection of military escorts due to violence from both local law enforcement and citizens.

bomb into the bus. The mob viciously beat the riders as they exited the burning bus. The protesters were then arrested despite having done nothing wrong. Even though their actions were legal, the protesters chose to stay in jail rather than accept bail.

A VERY VIOLENT REACTION

Whites who feared an integrated society had used violence against African Americans since the end of the Civil War. Sadly, most whites who committed violent acts against blacks were not prosecuted. Some law enforcement officials belonged to hate groups or sympathized with them and protected those of their own race. In some cases, the victims of violence were persecuted with beatings, jail time, or lynching.

Even peaceful protests attracted violent reactions. In March 1965, Martin Luther King Jr. led a march through Alabama, starting from the town of Selma. At the Alabama River, the marchers were met by police and told to turn back. When they refused, the police attacked with tear gas and clubs. More than fifty people

In 1965, Dr. Martin Luther King Jr. led a peaceful march from Montgomery to Selma, Alabama, to support and maintain voting rights for all black Americans.

were hospitalized. This unjustified reaction to nonviolent protest was seen on televisions around the world. The movement gained more support, especially from people who had not known how bad the conditions faced by blacks in the South were.

THE MOVEMENT GROWS

In 1960, African Americans made up only 10 percent of the total population. In order for real civil rights changes to occur, people outside of the black community would need to join the movement, too. The inclusion of white college students marked a major difference between the protests of the 1960s and those of earlier years. In 1960, a group of students in Ann Arbor, Michigan, formed Students for a Democratic Society (SDS). SDS supported groups such as CORE and SNCC and also protested the Vietnam War.

Integration in the activist ranks was also a key to the rapid growth of the civil rights movement. It created a community that crossed racial lines. One of the biggest integrated gatherings of the civil rights movement was the March on Washington in

The peaceful protests of the civil rights movement helped inspire the largely white antiwar movement of the 1960s.

August 1963. More than two hundred thousand people marched to the Lincoln Memorial to demand peace and equality. A highlight of the march was Martin Luther King Jr.'s famous "I Have a Dream" speech.

THE CIVIL RIGHTS ACT OF 1964

The most important law passed during civil rights movement was the Civil Rights Act of 1964. Signed into law by President Lyndon B. Johnson, it banned segregation in public places and employment discrimination on the basis of "race, color, religion, sex or national origin." This law overruled the discriminatory state legislation and led to the passage of other laws that gave all Americans an equal chance for freedom and success.

The Civil Right Act of 1964 had been proposed by President Johnson's predecessor, John F. Kennedy. But, fearing change, many southern congressmen fought against its passage for over two years. Despite the opposition, the Civil Rights Act of 1964 became law and set the stage for additional legislation. It is difficult to overstate the act's importance. In the words of Martin Luther King Jr., it was a "second emancipation."

President John F. Kennedy was a vocal supporter of civil rights legislation—he mentioned it as early as 1960 during his campaign for president. He was assassinated before the Civil Rights Act of 1964 was passed.

GETTING MORE RESULTS

The Civil Rights Act of 1964 was a huge milestone for civil rights, but one piece of legislation was not able to solve all of the problems surrounding the thorny issue of equality. More legislation was enacted over the next few years that provided increased protections for African Americans.

The Voting Rights Act of 1965 prohibited racial discrimination against African American voters that had been legalized by Jim Crow laws. Requirements for voting such as literacy tests and property ownership were now illegal.

The Immigration and Nationality Services Act of 1965 targeted unfair immigration laws, such as those that allowed fewer Asians and Africans to enter the United States than white Europeans.

Voting has always been one of the best ways to make changes in a democracy. Despite heavy opposition, the Voting Rights Act of 1965 was a huge step toward an equal voice for black Americans.

The Fair Housing Act of 1968 put a stop to discrimination in the sale and rental of housing based on sex, religion, race, and ethnicity.

These laws helped bury the senseless prejudice of Jim Crow and made it easier for all citizens to live productive and peaceful lives.

SIT-INS OUTSIDE OF THE CIVIL RIGHTS MOVEMENT

Although the sit-in was popularized during the civil rights movement, it has been used in other movements to seek better social and economic conditions for all people. In 1970, more than one hundred women held a sit-in at the offices of the *Ladies' Home Journal* to protest hiring practices and low salaries. The magazine's contents focused on housework and fashion but no other more serious subjects. Many staff members were male, and the protesters believed that a magazine dedicated to women and their interests should be reflected in hiring. In 2016, Democratic members of Congress held a twenty-five-hour sit-in on the floor of the House of Representatives to demand stricter gun control laws. They were inspired by a tragic mass shooting in Orlando, Florida. The sit-in did not change policy, but, like sit-ins of the past, it did bring attention to one of the most important issues of our time.

The sit-in by Democratic members of Congress in 2016 was intended to force a vote on new gun control laws after numerous mass shootings.

AFTER THE CIVIL RIGHTS MOVEMENT

Violent reactions to the civil rights movement continued through the mid-1960s. The assassinations of President John F. Kennedy in 1963 and Dr. Martin Luther King Jr. in 1965 demonstrated how much anger and resistance to desegregation and equality there was among whites. More and more civil rights activists began to feel that if nonviolence was always met with violence, then violence in retaliation was acceptable. Younger voices grew more impatient with each violent act against activists. In 1966, SNCC president Stokely Carmichael said in a speech: "We have to organize ourselves to speak for each other. That's Black Power." However, many members of the Black Power movement did not favor violence, which they saw as harmful to the struggle for equality for all Americans.

Thanks to the leaders of the early civil rights movement, the next generation of protesters and activists were inspired to continue marching—and staging sit-ins—for universal justice.

The concept of justice is at the heart of democracy. Nonviolent protests demanding that justice are sometimes necessary for the good of our nation as a whole.

GLOSSARY

abolish To end or stop something.

activist A person who uses different types of protests to change social or economic conditions.

civil disobedience To refuse to obey a law or ruling in order to change unjust policies.

civil liberties Personal rights and freedoms that all citizens deserve.

civil rights The rights of freedom, equality, and equal opportunity that citizens have in a society.

discrimination To treat a person unfairly because of his or her race, gender, religion, or ethnicity.

emancipate To set free.

ethnicity A shared religious, cultural, or national background.

hate group An organization that supports or uses violence or hatred against people of different ethnicities.

integration To bring people from different groups together as equal members of a society.

lynching The execution of a person by a mob, usually by hanging.

philosophy A certain type of thinking about the world and reality.

plantation A piece of land used for the growing and sale of crops such as cotton or sugarcane.

prejudice A negative opinion made without facts or research.

reinforce To support or back up.

retaliate To fight back.

riot A violent civil disorder performed by a large group of people.

segregation Setting a particular group of people apart based on race or gender.

strike To refuse to work until needs or desires are addressed.

viewpoint A certain way of looking at an idea or concept.

Center for Nonviolent Communication (CNVC)
9301 Indian School Road NE, Suite 204
Albuquerque, NM 87112-2861
(505) 244-4041
Website: http://www.cnvc.org
Facebook: @centerfornonviolentcommunication
The CNVC works to "help people peacefully and effectively resolve conflicts in personal, organizational, and political settings."

Greenpeace Canada
33 Cecil Street
Toronto, ON M5T 1N1
Canada
(416) 597-8408
Website: http://www.greenpeace.org/canada/en/home
Facebook: @greenpeace.canada
Instagram: @greenpeace.canada
Twitter: @greenpeaceCA
This organization that strives to protect the environment as well as spread the principles of nonviolence across the globe.

Metta Center for Nonviolence
PO Box 98
Petaluma, CA 94953
(707) 774-6299
Website: http://mettacenter.org
Facebook: @MettaCenterforNonviolence
Twitter: @MettaCenter

The center's goal is to "inspire, educate, and support the practice of nonviolence," to bring about global change and equality.

National Museum of African American History & Culture
14th Street and Constitution Avenue
Washington, DC 20001
(844) 750-3012
Website: https://nmaahc.si.edu
Facebook: @NMAAHC
Instagram: @NMAAHC
Twitter: @NMAAHC
The museum is one the nineteen museums and galleries that make up the Smithsonian Institution.

Resource Center for Nonviolence (RCNV)
612 Ocean Street
Santa Cruz, CA 95060
(831) 423-1626
Website: http://www.rcnv.org
Facebook: @rcnvsc
Twitter: @RCNV1
Instagram: @the_rcnv
The RCNV "promotes the practice of nonviolent social change."

Websites

Because of the changing nature of internet links, Rosen Publishing has developed an online list of websites related to the subject of this book. This site is updated regularly. Please use this link to access this list:

http://www.rosenlinks.com/SCRM/Protest

FOR FURTHER READING

Bass, Hester. *Seeds of Freedom: The Peaceful Integration of Huntsville, Alabama*. Somerville, MA: Candlewick Press, 2010.

Dear, John. *The Nonviolent Life*. Corvallis, OR: Pace e Bene Press, 2013.

Herr, Melody. *Sitting for Equal Service: Lunch Counter Sit-Ins, United States, 1960s.* Minneapolis, MN: Twenty-First Century Books, 2010.

Hoose, Phillip. *Claudette Colvin: Twice Toward Justice.* New York, NY: Square Fish Books, 2010.

King, Dr. Martin Luther Jr. *A Time to Break Silence: The Essential Works of Martin Luther King, Jr., for Students.* Nassau, Bahamas: Turtleback, 2013.

Kurlansky, Mark. *Nonviolence: The History of a Dangerous Idea*. New York, NY: Random House Publishing Group, 2008.

Leacock, Elspeth, and Susan Buckley. *Turning 15 on the Road to Freedom: My Story of the 1865 Selma Voting Rights March*. New York, NY: Dial Books, 2015.

Levine, Ellen S. *Freedom's Children: Young Civil Rights Activists Tell Their Own Stories*. London, UK: Puffin Books, 2010.

Levinson, Cynthia. *We've Got a Job: The 1963 Birmingham Children's March*. Atlanta, GA: Peachtree Publishers, 2015.

Nagler, Michael N. *The Nonviolence Handbook: A Guide for Practical Action*. Oakland, CA: Barrett-Koehler Publishers, 2014.

Partridge, Elizabeth. *Marching for Freedom: Walk Together, Children, and Don't You Grow Weary*. New York, NY: Viking Books for Young Readers, 2009.

Pinckney, Andrea Davis. *Sit-In: How Four Friends Stood Up By Sitting Down*. New York, NY: Little, Brown Books for Young Readers, 2010.

Quinn, Jason. *Gandhi: My Life Is My Message.* New Delhi, India. Campfire, 2014.

BIBLIOGRAPHY

Aretha, David. *Sit-ins and Freedom Rides*. Greensboro, NC: Morgan Reynolds Publishing, 2009.

Bausam, Ann. *The March Against Fear: The Last Great Walk of the Civil Rights Movement and the Emergence of Black Power.* Washington, DC: National Geographic Children's Books, 2017.

Bynum, Thomas. *NAACP Youth and the Fight for Black Freedom, 1936–1965*. Knoxville, TN: University of Tennessee Press, 2013.

Carson, Clayborne, et. al. *Eyes on the Prize Civil Rights Reader: Documents, Speeches, and Firsthand Accounts from the Black Freedom Struggle*. New York, NY: Penguin Books, 1991.

Cassie, Ron. "And Service for All: Sixty Years ago, Morgan State College Students Staged the First Successful Lunch-counter Sit-ins." *Baltimore Magazine*, January 2015.

Coates, Ken. *Work-ins, Sit-ins and Industrial Democracy.* Nottingham, UK: Spokesman Press, 1981.

Douglass, Frederick. *Narrative of the Life of Frederick Douglass*. Mineral, NY: Dover Publications, 1995.

Hurst, Rodney L. Sr. *It Was Never About a Hot Dog and a Coke! A Personal Account of the 1960 Sit-in Demonstrations in Jacksonville, Florida and Ax Handle Saturday.* Livermore, CA: WingSpan Press, 2008.

Morgan, Iwan, and Philip Davis. *From Sit-ins to SNCC: The Student Civil Rights Movement in the 1960s*. Gainesville, FL: University Press of Florida, 2013.

O'Brien, M.J. *We Shall Not Be Moved: The Jackson Woolworth's Sit-In and the Movement It Inspired*. Foreword by Julian Bond. Jackson, MS: University Press of Mississippi, 2014.

Wolff, Miles. *Lunch at the 5 & 10: The Greensboro Sit-Ins: A Contemporary History*. New York, NY: Stein and Day, 1970.

INDEX

About the Author

Kerry Hinton is a writer who has always had a keen interest in social justice and civil rights. Thanks to the firsthand experiences of his parents and grandparents under the harsh conditions of Jim Crow in the South and discrimination in the North, he has enjoyed a lifelong engagement with the principles and ideas behind the civil rights movement. He enjoys the films and music of the Black Power movement and lives in Brooklyn, New York.

PHOTO CREDITS

Cover, p. 1 Shel Hershorn/Archive Photos/Getty Images; pp. 3, 42, 43, 45, 46, 47 Onur Ersin/Shutterstock.com; p. 5 Suzanne Tucker /Shutterstock.com; pp. 4, 8, 12, 16, 18, 20, 22, 24, 26, 28, 30, 32, 34, 36, 38, 40, back cover Sergey Kamshylin/Shutterstock.com; pp. 6–7 d_odin/Shutterstock.com; pp. 9, 10, 14–15 Everett Historical /Shutterstock.com; p. 13 Flip Schulke Archives/Corbis Premium Historical/Getty Images; pp. 17, 19, 25, 27, 33 Bettmann/Getty Images; p. 21 David Frent/Corbis Historical/Getty Images; p. 23 Howard Sochurek/The LIFE Picture Collection/Getty Images; p. 29 Paul Schutzer/The LIFE Picture Collection/Getty Images; p. 31 Robert Abbott Sengstacke/Archive Photos/Getty Images; p. 35 thatsmymop/Shutterstock.com; p. 37 MPI/Archive Photos /Getty Images; p. 39 Allison Shelley/Getty Images; p. 41 r.classen /Shutterstock.com.

Design: Nelson Sá; Editor and Photo Researcher: Xina M. Uhl